T0198811

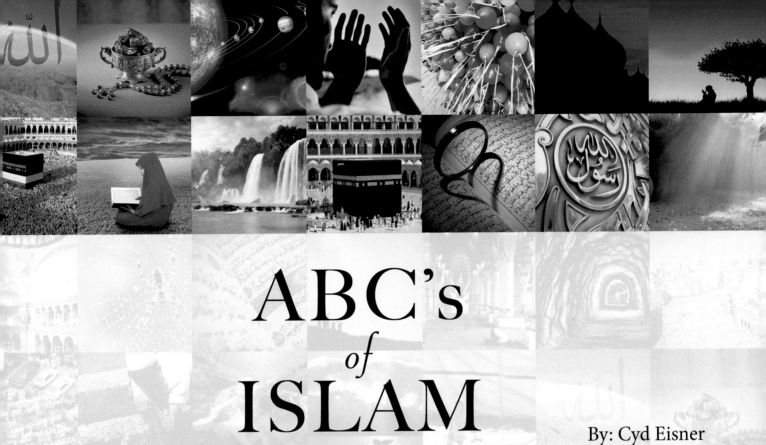

ABC's
of
ISLAM

By: Cyd Eisner

AuthorHouse™
1663 Liberty Drive
Bloomington, IN 47403
www.authorhouse.com
Phone: 833-262-8899

Because of the dynamic nature of the Internet, any web addresses or links contained in this book may have changed since publication and may no longer be valid. The views expressed in this work are solely those of the author and do not necessarily reflect the views of the publisher, and the publisher hereby disclaims any responsibility for them.

This book is printed on acid-free paper.

Author: Cyd Eisner
Graphic Designers: Lamya El-Shacke and Tarek Reda
Cover Design: Lamya El-Shacke

ISBN: 978-1-4772-7858-1 (sc)
        978-1-4772-7859-8 (e)

Library of Congress Control Number: 2012919022

Print information available on the last page.

Published by AuthorHouse 01/19/2021

author HOUSE®

ABC's
of
ISLAM

By: Cyd Eisner

This book is dedicated to my loving mother who taught me the abc's of life. There are not enough words or actions that show my love, thanks and appreciation. If it weren't for your hard work, tough love and confidence I don't know where I would be today. Thank you for directing me to make the proper choices in life. You are one of a kind and I am blessed to have you as my mother.

A

is for

Allah

The One and
Only God. The
Creator of the
Heavens, the
Earth, and
all that is in
between.

B

is for

Bismillah

In the name of
Allah (SWT) the
Most Gracious,
the Most Merciful.
A Muslim should
say this before
doing anything
throughout
their day.

C

is for

Creator

The heavens and the earth were created in six days. Look closely to the sun, moon and stars and you will never doubt the existence of the Creator.

D

is for

Dua'a

Dua'a (supplication) is an action in which Muslims ask Allah (SWT) to provide ourselves or someone else with something good or beneficial.

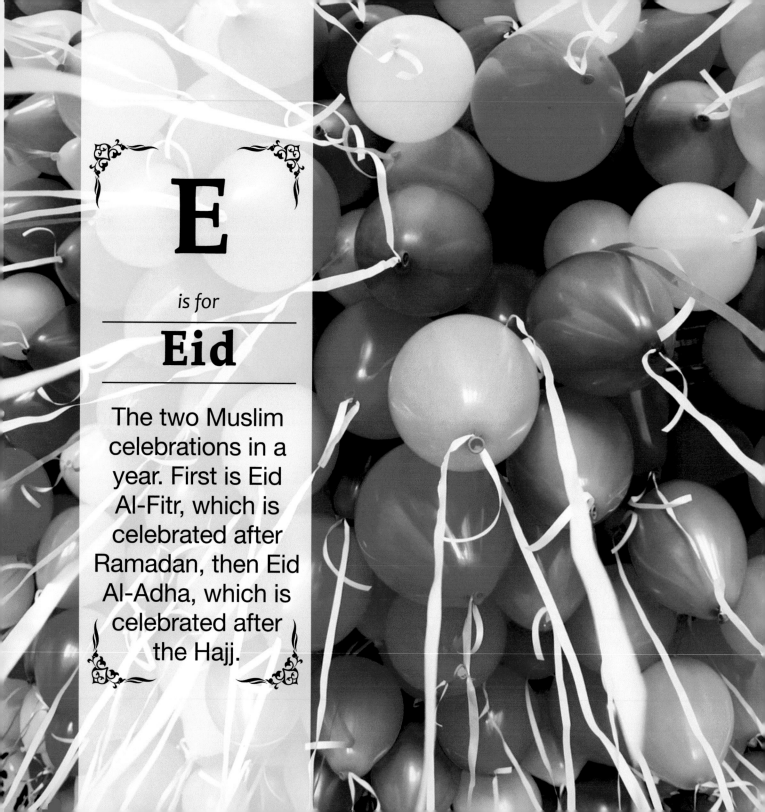

E

is for

Eid

The two Muslim celebrations in a year. First is Eid Al-Fitr, which is celebrated after Ramadan, then Eid Al-Adha, which is celebrated after the Hajj.

F

is for

Five Pillars of Islam

The five pillars of Islam are the foundations of Muslim life. They are: Shahadah, Salah, Sawm, Zakah and Hajj.

G

is for

Gracious

Allah (SWT)
is gracious
to those who
wholeheartedly
repent.

H

is for

Hajj

For those who are physically and financially capable, the obligatory pilgrimage to Makkah that a Muslim must perform at least once in his or her lifetime.

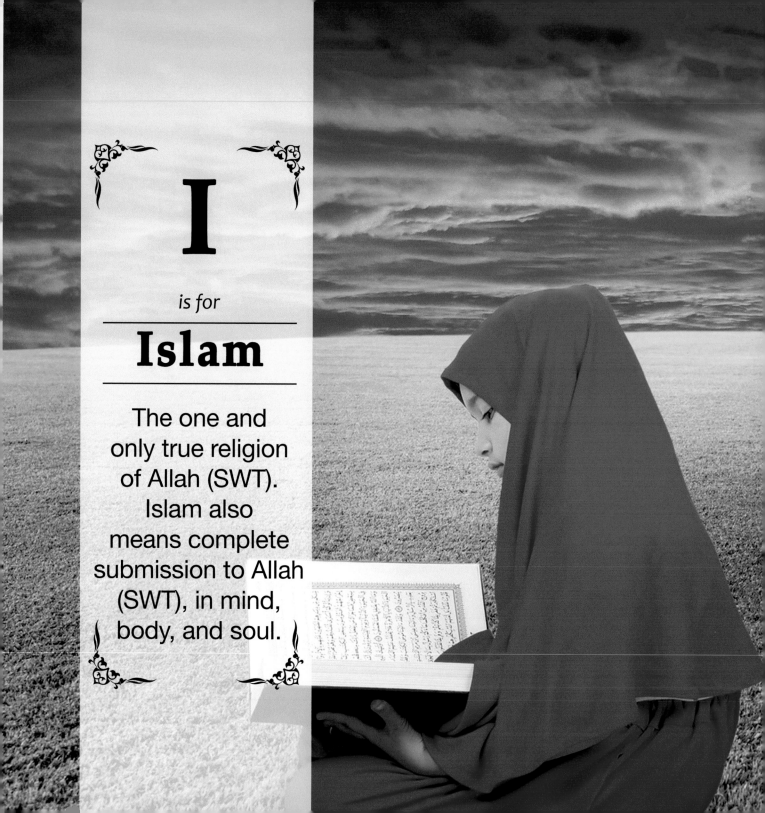

I

is for

Islam

The one and only true religion of Allah (SWT). Islam also means complete submission to Allah (SWT), in mind, body, and soul.

J

is for

Jannah

A paradise in the afterlife to all the Muslims who follow Allah's (SWT) religion and who follow the way of Prophet Muhammad (SAW).

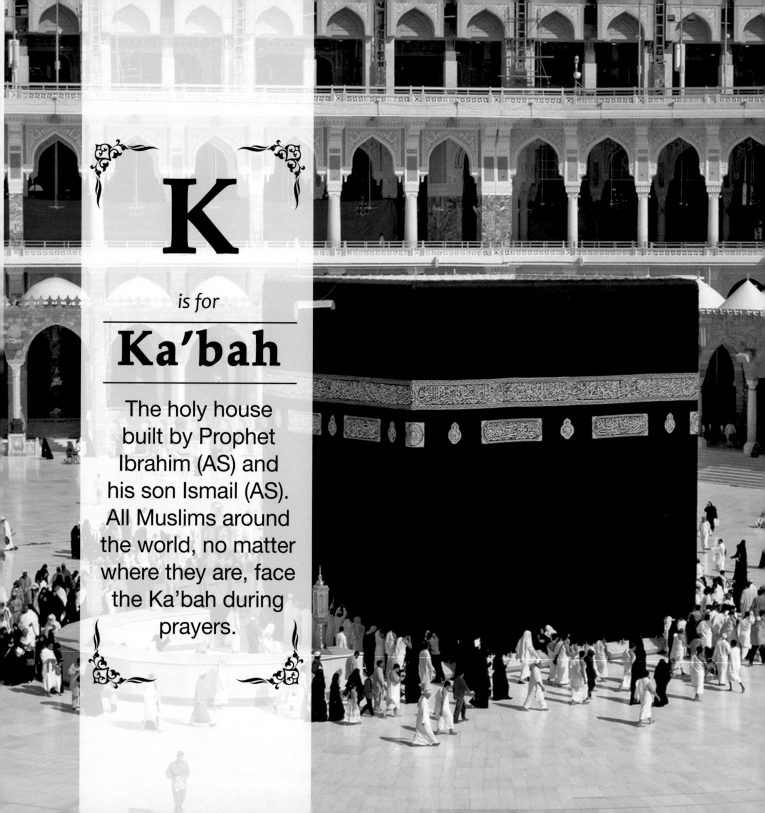

K

is for

Ka'bah

The holy house built by Prophet Ibrahim (AS) and his son Ismail (AS). All Muslims around the world, no matter where they are, face the Ka'bah during prayers.

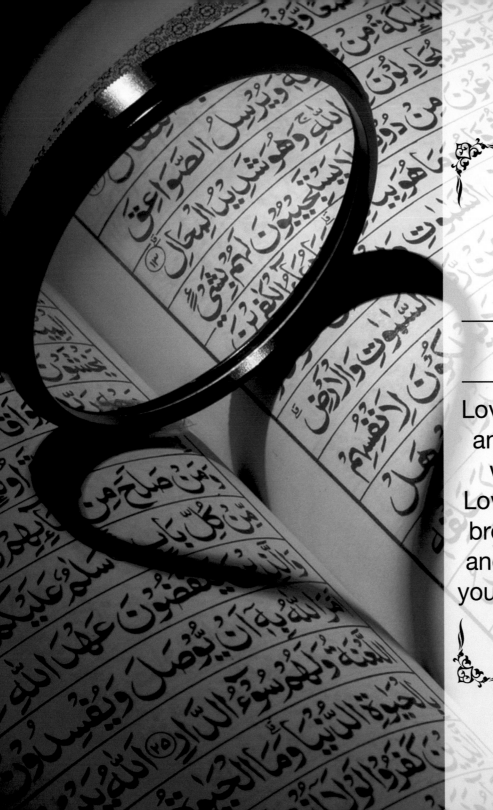

L

is for

Love

Love your parents
and Allah (SWT)
will love you.
Love your Muslim
brothers, sisters,
and neighbors as
you yourself would
want to
be loved.

M

is for

Muhammad

The teacher of
Islam — Allah's
(SWT) final Prophet
and Messenger —
sent as a mercy to
all of mankind.

N

is for

Noor

The angels are created from Noor (Light).

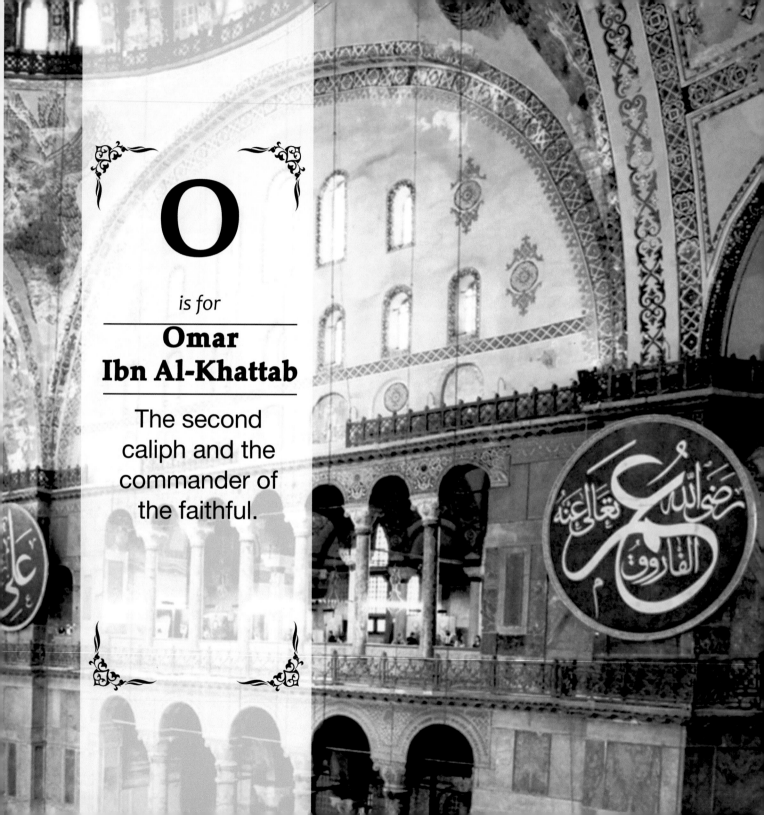

O

is for

Omar
Ibn Al-Khattab

The second
caliph and the
commander of
the faithful.

P

is for

Patience

The state of acting calm and intelligent under difficult circumstances. One of the most important characteristics one needs to enter Jannah.

Q

is for

Quran

The last revelation to mankind sent to Prophet Muhammad (SAW), also known as the miracle of Prophet Muhammad (SAW). Still to this day in its original form, the Holy Quran is protected by Allah (SWT).

R

is for

Ramadan

Ramadan is the holiest of all months. All Muslims must fast from Fajr (Dawn) to Maghrib (Sunset).
It is the month in which the Quran was revealed to Prophet Muhammad (SAW).

S

is for

Salah

Prayers performed five times a day to worship Allah (SWT). One must pray to enter Jannah.

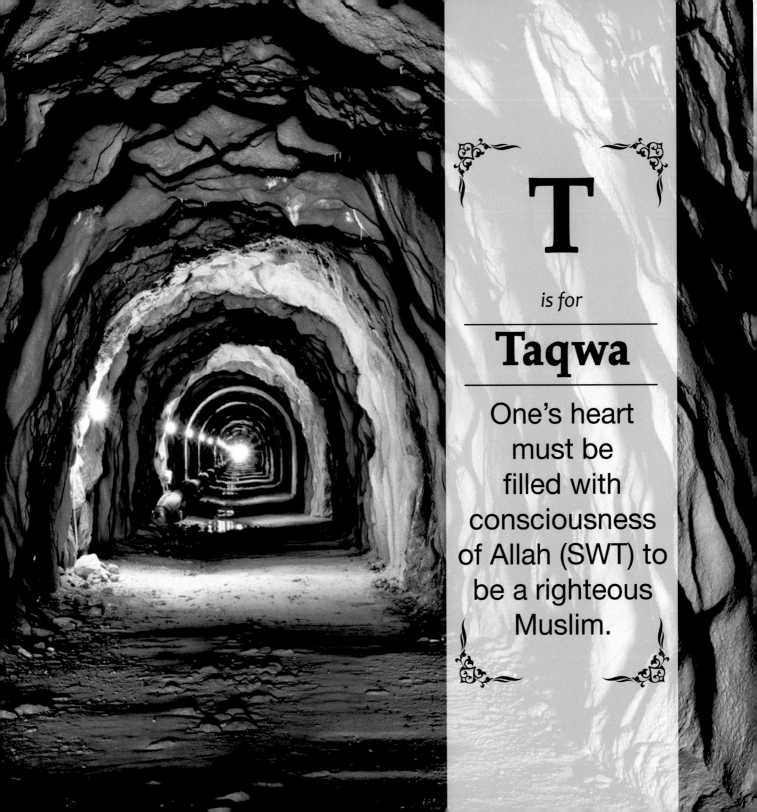

T

is for

Taqwa

One's heart must be filled with consciousness of Allah (SWT) to be a righteous Muslim.

U

is for

Ummah

The nation of Prophet Muhammad (SAW), which is unified as one global community.

V

is for

Virtue

Virtue is the practice of moral excellence. This will help unite the Muslim Ummah and will inspire us to acquire and put to use better behaviors.

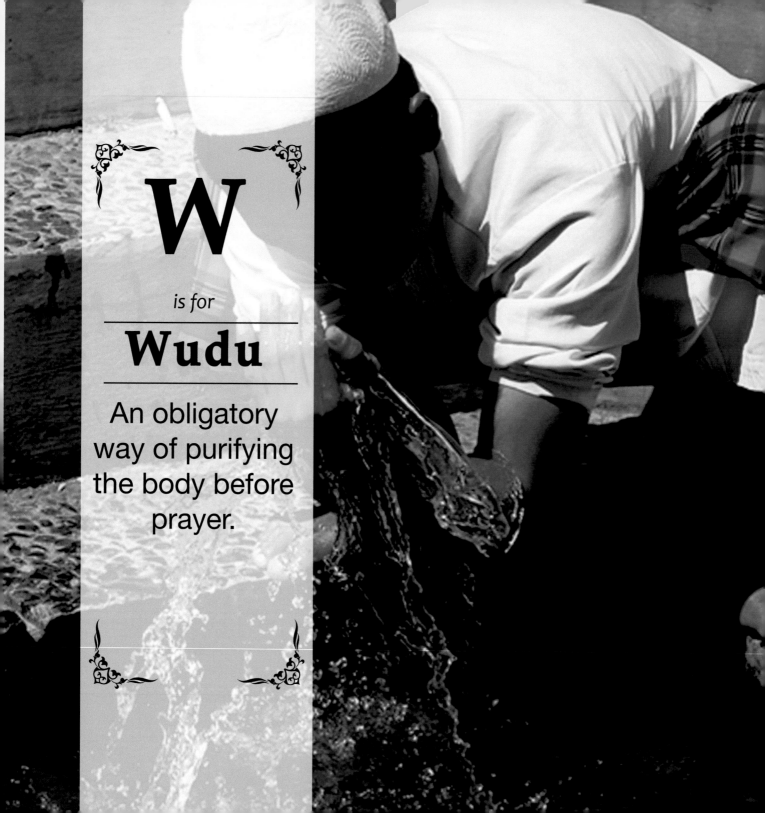

W

is for

Wudu

An obligatory way of purifying the body before prayer.

X

is for

eXhilarate

Reading Quran stimulates our Iman and is invigorating for the mind, body and soul.

Y

is for

Yunus

The Prophet
who supplicated
(made Dua'a) to
Allah (SWT) in
the belly of
a whale.

Z

is for

Zakah

An obligatory charity that is given to the poor.

May this book reassure you of Allah's (SWT) Infinite Power and strengthen your love for Him. May it be a light in times of hardship and may it increase your Iman and your Islam. May this ABC book guide you through the ABC's of life. Ameen.

Glossary

SWT: Spelled out in the English transliteration, "*Subhanahu wa ta'ala*" means Glorified and Exalted is He. This is the expression said after saying Allah's (God's) name. A Muslim should say this out of respect of Allah and to display proper etiquette for the Almighty.

AS: Spelled out in English transliteration, "*Alayhi al-salam*" means peace and blessings upon him. This is the expression said after saying the names of all the Prophets. One can say AS or SAW. A Muslim should say this out of respect for them and to display proper etiquette.

SAW: Spelled out in English transliteration, "*Sall Allahu alay-hi-wa-salam*" means may Allah (SWT) honor him and grant him peace. This is the expression said after saying the names of all the Prophets. One can say AS or SAW. SAW is primarily said after saying Prophet Muhammad's name because he is the last and final prophet and because of a certain verse in the Quran that is mentioned specifically for him. "Verily God and His angels bless the Prophet! O you who believe, send blessings unto him and greet him with a salutation worthy of respect."[1] Muslims should say this out of respect for them and to display proper etiquette.

Eid Al-Fitr: The celebration to express delight and gratitude to Allah (SWT) to mark the end of Ramadan, the month long fast of no food and water from dawn till dusk.

Eid Al-Adha: "Festival of Sacrifice" is the celebration to mark the end of Hajj in which an animal is sacrificed, then the meat is given and distributed amongst the poor, neighbors and friends.

Caliph: Successor to lead the Muslim nation after Prophet Muhammad (SAW).

Iman: Means faith.

The five pillars of Islam:
1. Shahadah or the Islamic profession of faith/Oneness of God, "There is no god but Allah (SWT), and Muhammad (SAW) is his messenger"
2. Salah or prayer
3. Sawm or fasting
4. Zakah or an obligatory charity that is given to the poor
5. Hajj or pilgrimage

---

1. *The Quran, Surah 33:56*

About the Author

Cyd Eisner recently began writing books for Muslim children of all ages and for children of all faiths in an effort to encourage better understanding and cultivate an appreciation of the Islamic religion. Cyd converted from Judaism to Islam in 1999. She received her B.A. from the University of Hartford in 2004, and she now lives in Virginia with her husband and five children.

Printed in the United States
By Bookmasters